KAREL HUSA

POSTCARD FROM HOME

for Alto Saxophone and Piano

(Score and Part)

AMP 8145

First printing: February 1999

ISBN 0-634-00027-6

Associated Music Publishers, Inc.

DISTRIBUTED BY

HAL•LEONARD®
CORPORATION
7777 W. BLUEMOUND RD. P.O. BOX 13819 MILWAUKEE, WI 53213

KAREL HUSA

POSTCARD FROM HOME

for Alto Saxophone and Piano

(Score and Part)

Associated Music Publishers, Inc.

DISTRIBUTED BY

HAL•LEONARD®

PROGRAM NOTE

Postcard from Home was composed in 1997 at the kind suggestion of saxophonist John Sampen. It is inspired by two Moravian folk melodies. The first is treated as a short recitative, expressing joyful singing in the mountains, with echoes; the second, resembling an aria, is about a young man leaving his country with great expectations, yet wondering if he will be remembered when he returns.

—KAREL HUSA

duration: ca. 4 minutes

premiere performance: August 1, 1997 in Taipei, Taiwan
John Sampen, saxophone; Marilyn Schrude, piano

Alto Saxophone in E♭

POSTCARD FROM HOME

Karel Husa

Ad lib.
(♩ = ca. 48)

Andante (♩ = 58)

POSTCARD FROM HOME

Karel Husa

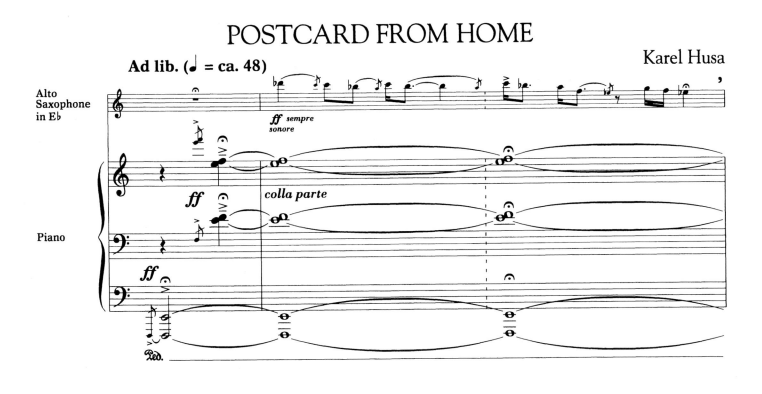

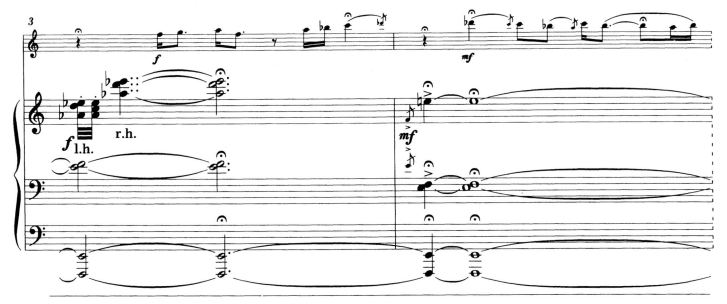

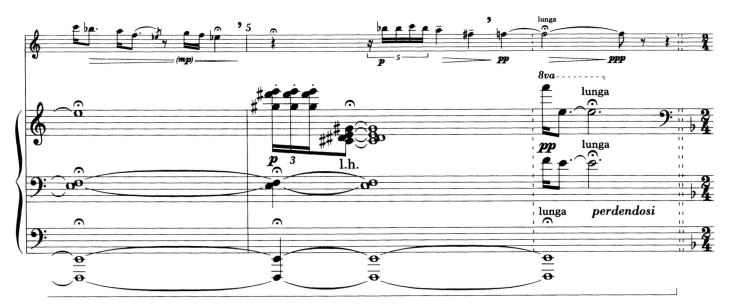

attacca

Andante (♩ = 58)

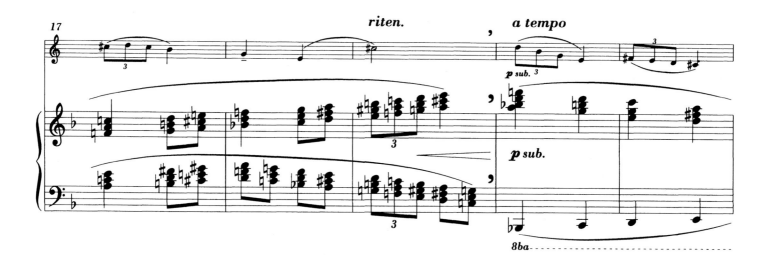

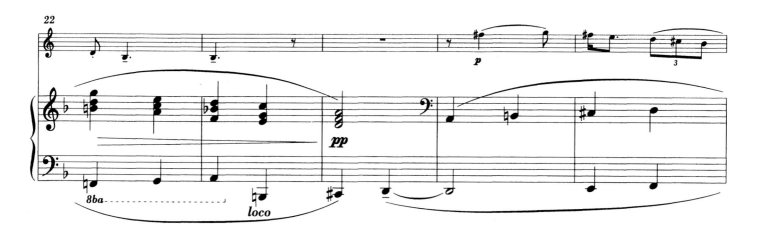

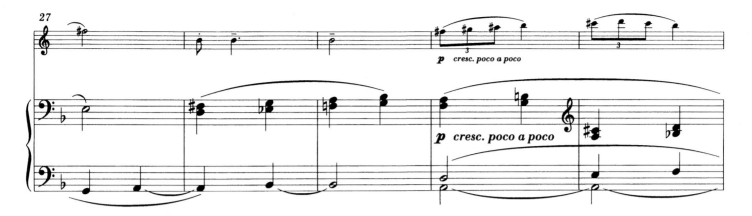

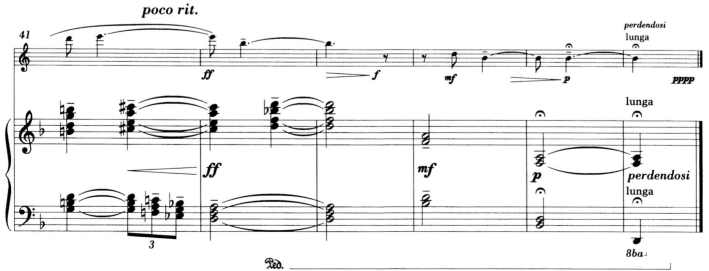